My papery parcel
will split open
and I'll wriggle out
into the sunshine!
When my wings are
dry, I'll fly about
and drink nectar
from flowers.

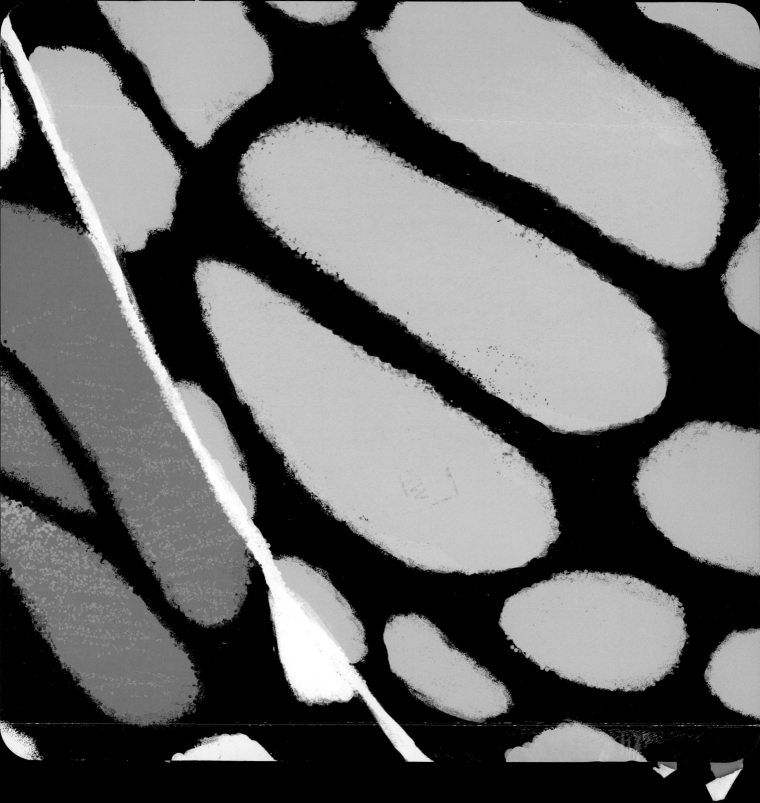

A
BUTTERFLY!

1. When I'm ready, I'll lay my tiny eggs on a leaf.

2. They'll hatch into little cate that will eat and grow.

3. And grow until they are MUCH bigger.

4. Then they'll each make a small papery parcel and hang under a leaf by a silken thread...

ready to be a butterfly!

I'm newly born, pink and white
and blind. I'm so small you could
hold me in one hand.

WHAT WILL I BE?

1. I'll go seal hunting with my mum on the frozen sea. When I'm older I can hunt seals on my own.

2. I'll grow and grow until my feet are as big as dinner plates!

3. Then, one winter, I'll make a den under the snow.

4. And have pink and white babies of my own!

I'm as round and white as a ping-pong ball. I lie underneath warm sand.

WHAT WILL I BE?

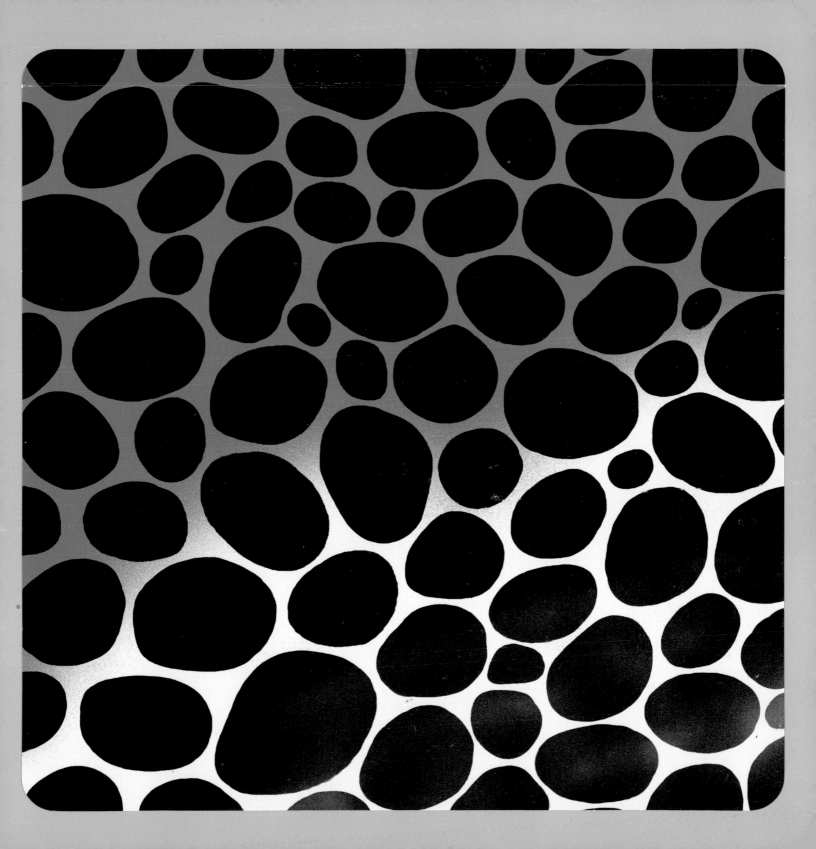

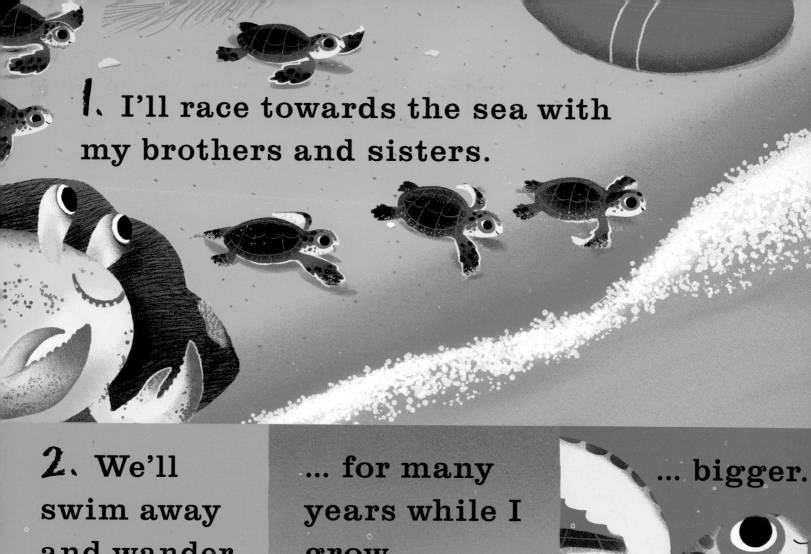

1. I'll race towards the sea with my brothers and sisters.

2. We'll swim away and wander the sea ...

... for many years while I grow ...

... bigger.

3. When I'm very big, I'll come back to the beach where I was born.

4. I'll lay eggs, round and white as ping-pong balls in the warm sand.

I'm a black dot in a blob
of jelly, floating in the pond.

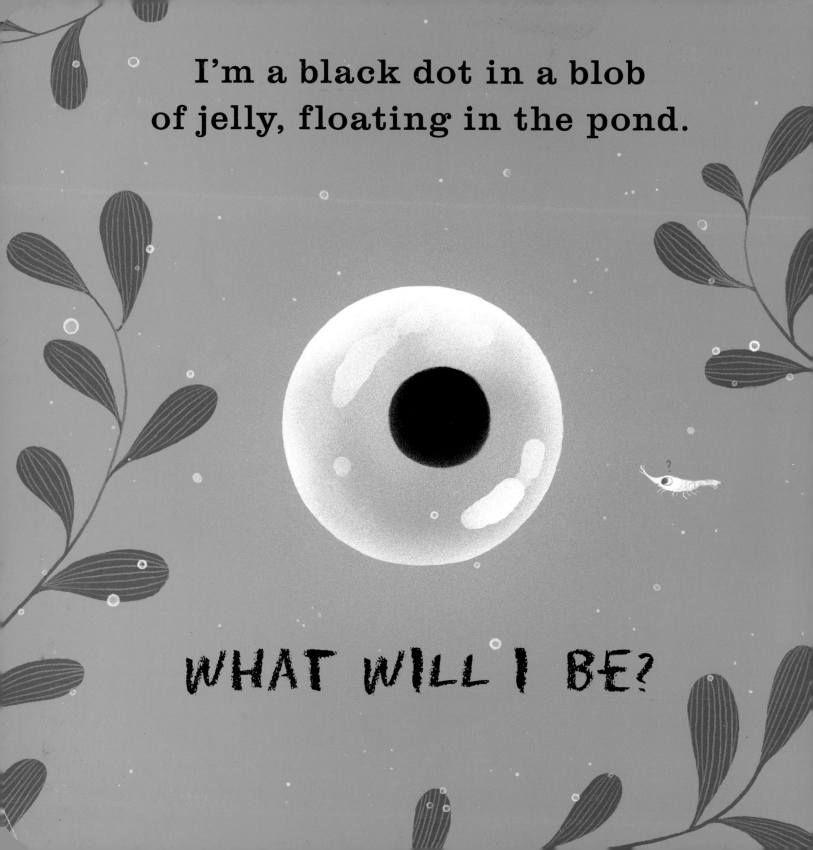

WHAT WILL I BE?

1. I'll swim around the pond and grow front legs.

2. Then I'll grow back ones.

3. I'll lose my tail, and turn into a teeny frog so I can hop away.

4. When I've grown much, MUCH **bigger** I'll come back to the pond to lay lots of eggs like dots in blobs of jelly.

I'm speckled and spotted
and smaller than a grape.

WHAT WILL I BE?

2. Then my feathers will sprout.

3. Soon I'll flap my wings and fly away.

4. And next year I'll make a nest for my own speckled, spotted eggs.

What will they be?
Match the colours
to find out.

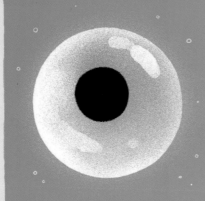

And what about this baby? What will **HE** be?

First published 2012 by Walker Books Ltd
87 Vauxhall Walk, London SE11 5HJ

1 3 5 7 9 10 8 6 4 2

Text © 2012 Nicola Davies
Illustrations © 2012 Marc Boutavant

The right of Nicola Davies and Marc Boutavant to be
identified as author and illustrator respectively of
this work has been asserted by them in accordance
with the Copyright, Designs and Patents Act 1988

This book has been typeset in Print, Clarendon T
and Eraser

Printed in China

British Library Cataloguing in Publication Data:
a catalogue record for this book is available
from the British Library.

ISBN 978-1-4063-2813-4

www.walker.co.uk